Walk the Talk
1 Peter

Transformation—the process of becoming holy—begins in your mind.

A 7-session study

BY STEVE MAY, WITH JOHANNAH REARDON

CHRISTIAN
Bible Studies

Walk the Talk: 1 Peter

Transformation—the process of becoming holy—begins in your mind.

From Christian Bible Studies

Copyright © 2018 | Christianity Today

Published by Christianity Today,
465 Gundersen Dr., Carol Stream, IL 60188

Printed in the U.S.A.

ChristianBibleStudies.com
ChristianityToday.org

All rights reserved.

Unless otherwise specified, Scripture taken from the Holy Bible, New International Version®, NIV®. Copyright © 1973, 1978, 1984, 2011 by Biblica, Inc.™ Used by permission of Zondervan. All rights reserved worldwide. Zondervan.com

ChristianBibleStudies.com Team
Associate Publisher: Amy Jackson
Associate Editor: Emily Lund
Design: Jillian Hathaway
Marketing: Kristen Cloyd

WRITTEN BY STEVE MAY, WITH JOHANNAH REARDON

CHRISTIAN Bible Studies

Table of Contents

- **7** *How to Use This Study*
- **9** *Overview of 1 Peter*
- **13** SESSION 1: *The Battle for Holiness*
- **23** SESSION 2: *When I Don't Feel Like Being Good*
- **35** SESSION 3: *An Appetite for Being Good*
- **47** SESSION 4: *Refuse to Get Revenge*
- **61** SESSION 5: *Learn to Live in Peace*
- **71** SESSION 6: *Get Ready for a Rough Ride*
- **83** SESSION 7: *You're in Good Hands*
- **93** *Discussion Guide*

How to Use This Study

This Bible study is designed to be used either on your own or as part of a Bible study group. Each session has a Bible passage to read and several questions to answer. You'll find plenty of space to write down your thoughts along the way. Plus, you'll find specific application ideas and questions at the end of each session.

Move through the sessions at a pace that makes sense to you. For many, doing one session each week will make the most sense. This allows you to reflect on all the information you read. It also works well if you're meeting to discuss what you're learning with a Bible study group. At each weekly meeting, you can discuss what you've read in the week's session. That said, there are no rules! This is simply meant to be a tool to help you dig into God's Word and apply it in practical ways.

If you are using this as part of a Bible study group, be sure to use the discussion guide at the end of the book to guide your conversations. You'll find additional questions to ask and leader's notes to help you as you facilitate discussion. Alternatively, you can simply have group members discuss the answers to each session's questions when you gather.

We hope this tool helps you gain new insights from God's Word.

THE EDITORS OF CHRISTIAN BIBLE STUDIES

1 Peter

Why read this book?
Wouldn't it be great to be free of trouble? That's what we sometimes think. But 1 Peter shows us that difficulties and hardships don't have to wear us down. In fact, this letter teaches us that God can use difficulties to strengthen us. Knowing this can bring hope and reassurance that eternal life is God's ultimate purpose. Read 1 Peter to discover how faith, refined by suffering, can help us see the Lord more clearly. This is valuable advice for holding firm in difficult times.

Who wrote this book and why?
Peter, the apostle, saw that increasing hardship and persecution had caused some Christians to wonder if God had abandoned them. He wrote to encourage these believers, offering them hope and meaning in the midst of their suffering.

To whom was it written?
To believers scattered throughout the region of Asia Minor, in what is now Turkey.

Where and when was it written?
Probably in Rome, sometime between A.D. 60 and 64.

What was the background behind this book?
At first the Roman government had given Christians the same freedom of religion as the Jews. But as the rift between Jews and Christians grew, tolerance for Christianity faded. Roman policy was to ban problem religions, which were perceived as a threat to the stability of the empire. Christians began facing discrimination, acts of violence, arrest, and confiscation of property. Some were beginning to waver

in their faith. Others feared how much they would have to endure. Peter himself was imprisoned and beaten for his faith; thus he earned the right to address the subject of suffering.

What to look for in 1 Peter:
Reason for hope in the face of trouble and suffering. Take note of the encouraging news Peter sent to his readers.

FROM THE QUEST STUDY BIBLE (ZONDERVAN)

SESSION 1: THE BATTLE FOR HOLINESS

The Battle for Holiness

If you want to act holy, you have to learn to think holy.

Transformation—the process of becoming holy—begins in your mind. In 1 Peter we are challenged to live holy lives, and Peter shows us that the process of holy living begins with the way we think. Once we win that battle, we will begin to see changes in the way we live and the things we do. This study will explore how to begin that process.

Scripture:
1 Peter 1:13–16

Based on:
The sermon "The Battle for Holiness" by Steve May, *Preaching Today*

SESSION 1: THE BATTLE FOR HOLINESS

PART 1
Identify the Current Issue

If you shop Christian bookstores, you have probably noticed that different topics become hot for a time, and there are suddenly dozens of books related to whatever particular topic is in vogue. For example, in recent years prosperity, the Holy Spirit, the last days, demonology, and the New Age movement have been popular topics. However, there is one topic that is not likely to become trendy anytime soon, and that is holiness. Typically, books about holiness don't make it to the bestseller list. The subject is too uncomfortable—it's much easier to read the biography of a sports hero or a Christian novel.

Most preachers don't preach on holiness either. It's much easier to preach on forgiveness or grace. The 21th-century American church seems to be more concerned with being right than we are with living right.

Part of that may be because holiness seems out of reach for most of us. Paul warned us not to "think too highly" of ourselves, and most of us don't—in fact we go to the other extreme. We're much more comfortable saying, "I'm just a sinner saved by grace," than we are saying, "I am a holy saint of God." The fact is, both are true—or at least they can be, if we're willing to take the step toward holiness.

Just as we can claim forgiveness, mercy, healing, and blessings from God, we can also claim holiness—it is our birthright. God said in Leviticus, "You shall be holy," but this is often interpreted as a threat (i.e. "You shall be holy—or else!"). In reality it is a promise: "You shall be holy—because God will make you holy." Read Philippians 1:6.

For Christians, the problem is not so much a matter of wanting to be holy as it is winning the battle to be holy. Most of us aren't effective warriors. We are in the battle, but we're not sure why. Many of us don't know what it means to be holy or how to be holy.

The fact is, you can become holy in the next 30 seconds if you want to, because the word holy simply means "set apart for God's use." Do you want to be holy? Do you want to be set apart for his use? You can make that decision right now. Just dedicate yourself to him. Once you make that decision, you are holy—you are set apart for his service. It is that simple. From that decision you can begin the process of living a holy life.

Transformation—the process of becoming holy—begins in your mind. In 1 Peter we are challenged to live holy lives, and Peter shows us that the process of holy living begins with the way we think. Once we win that battle, we will begin to see changes in the way we live. If you want to act holy, you have to learn to think holy.

"Do not conform to the pattern of this world, but be transformed by the renewing of your mind. Then you will be able to test and approve what God's will is—his good, pleasing and perfect will" (Rom. 12:2).

PART 2
Discover the Eternal Principles

Read 1 Peter 1:13-16:

> Therefore, with minds that are alert and fully sober, set your hope on the grace to be brought to you when Jesus Christ is revealed at his coming. As obedient children, do not conform to the evil desires you had when you lived in ignorance. But just as he who called you is holy, so be holy in all you do; for it is written: "Be holy, because I am holy."

Teaching point one: To be holy, you must prepare your mind for action.

The King James Version renders verse 13 "Gird up the loins of your mind." This was a meaningful metaphor for first-century believers. In New Testament days men wore long robes that were quite a hindrance whenever a man needed to move quickly. Men also wore a belt around their waist,

SESSION 1: THE BATTLE FOR HOLINESS

so that when the occasion called for strenuous action, they could shorten the robe by pulling it up in the belt, giving them the freedom to run, fight, or whatever they needed to do. This was called "girding your loins."

When Peter said to gird up the loins of your mind, he meant, "Prepare yourself for strenuous mental activity. Your mind has become a battlefield; get ready to fight."

Every day we witness hundreds of events and images that attempt to influence the way we think. Some are clumsy and obvious, like a used-car-dealer commercial. Others, however, are slick and subtle, and if we are not careful we will find ourselves being influenced by the world, instead of by God's Word.

Years ago, when the personal computer was first introduced and millions of Americans were beginning to learn basic skills, one programmer coined a term that succinctly summarized computer technology: GIGO—"Garbage In, Garbage Out." If you write bad code into a program, you'll end up with a bad program. You get what you put in.

It's the same way with our minds. If we fill our minds with junk all day long, we'll end up thinking junk. If we fill our minds with the things of Christ, our lives will reflect the difference.

Holiness begins in your mind. For this reason, it is essential that we prepare our minds.

[Q] What are some practical ways we can prepare our minds for holiness?

Teaching point two: To be holy, you must think differently.

In verse 13, the NIV says to "be self-controlled." The King James Version reads, "Be sober." The Greek word translated sober can have two meanings, just like the English word. It can mean "not intoxicated," and it can mean "clearheaded." Either way, Peter is saying that if you are going to live a holy life, you have to keep your head on straight.

When a person becomes intoxicated, he loses the ability to reason; he loses perspective and tends to be ruled by his emotions rather than sound judgment. That's why it's dangerous when people drink and drive—they aren't capable of making good decisions. In the same way, Peter said, we must remain sober—not just free from intoxicating beverages, but free from intoxicating thoughts and emotions. If we live by our emotions, we will not be able to make good decisions. We have to separate our feelings from our thoughts.

That's what Peter meant when he said, "Be sober." He's saying, "Keep your head; don't be controlled by your emotions." Holiness begins in the mind, and for us to live holy lives there has to be that element of separation: we detach ourselves from our emotions, so that they don't have the power to control us, just as we detach ourselves from our possessions and the things of this world.

[Q] Which of the following best describes a holy life?
a. Never indulging in anything pleasurable
b. Never sinning
c. Only thinking about spiritual things
d. Being passionately in love with Christ, which colors the way you think and act

Why did you pick the statement you did? How does it affect the way you view holiness? What would be the difference between d. and the other choices? What is wrong with choices a.–c.?

SESSION 1: THE BATTLE FOR HOLINESS

Teaching point three: To be holy, you must learn to concentrate on God rather than your own efforts.

Have you ever watched small children play t-ball? There's something to be learned from them. One little girl didn't completely understand the rules and procedures of the game and seemed much too small to be on a baseball field, but she understood the game well enough to know that when her coach said, "Run," she was supposed to go to the next base. This little girl was focused. When she ran from first to second, her eyes were on nothing but second base. Buildings could have been falling down around her, helicopters could have landed in the outfield—she wouldn't have noticed. Her eyes were on second base.

This kind of concentration should characterize our approach to holy living. Peter said in verse 13, "set your hope fully on the grace to be given you when Jesus Christ is revealed."

The word translated *grace* is *charis*. It means "kindness shown to one who is undeserving." In New Testament days, *charis* was used to describe the kindness a master might show to a slave. It also describes the kindness that God shows to us. He is certainly not compelled to show kindness; he does it because he wants to. God shows kindness to us not because we are good, but because he is good. Our hope is in his goodness, not our own.

In evangelism a question is frequently asked: "If you were to die tonight and God asked, 'Why should I let you into my heaven?' what would your answer be?"

Whatever you say reveals where you have fixed your hope: "Because I am a good person ... because I go to church ... because I am a good husband/wife/father/mother ..." and so on. If this is your answer, then it indicates that you have placed your hope in your own goodness, and that is shaky ground. Our only true hope is God's grace. We cannot learn to live holy until we take our eyes off ourselves and concentrate on God. He should be the center of our attention.

[Q] Why must we have God's grace to live a holy life? Why are our own efforts doomed to fail?

PART 3
Apply Your Findings

There is a story about a college professor who told his students on the first day of class, "I've given you all an A. Now, learn all you can about the subject." In a sense, that is what God does for us. Hebrews 10:10 says, "We have been made holy through the sacrifice of the body of Jesus Christ once for all."

He has already made us holy. Our sins are forgiven, and we are clean. It is now up to us to apply holiness to our lives. Holiness begins in the mind. We have to prepare our minds for the battle for holiness, separate our thoughts from our emotions, and fix our eyes on God's grace.

SESSION 1: THE BATTLE FOR HOLINESS

[Q] What one thing will you do this week to prepare your mind for the battle of holiness?

SESSION 2: WHEN I DON'T FEEL LIKE BEING GOOD

When I Don't Feel Like Being Good

Being good makes sense.

This study discusses what is a split-second decision—whether in any given moment you do the right or the wrong thing. Our goal is to get good at being good. This means learning to live a life of integrity. To put it another way, it's about learning to become obedient to God. Integrity and obedience go hand in hand.

Scripture:
1 Peter 1:17–25

Based on:
The sermon "What If I Don't Feel Like Being Good?" by Steve May, *Preaching Today*

SESSION 2: WHEN I DON'T FEEL LIKE BEING GOOD

PART 1
Identify the Current Issue

Being good means living a life that is consistently obedient to God's will—choosing to do the right thing day in, day out.

Being good may be easy to define, but it's not always easy to do. By our very nature we don't always want to do what we know we should. The choice to obey is a split-second decision, and it is always our choice. There is not a sermon you can hear, a church you can attend, a seminar you can go to, or a self-help book you can read that will compel you to act with integrity in any given situation. It is your choice. However, there are things behind the scenes of every choice you make—things you think about and believe—that either empower you or cause you to fail to act with integrity.

So what if you don't feel like being good? Then you need to remember that being good makes good sense, and build the necessary foundation to develop a habit of obedience.

PART 2
Discover the Eternal Principles

Read 1 Peter 1:17-25:

> Since you call on a Father who judges each person's work impartially, live out your time as foreigners here in reverent fear. For you know that it was not with perishable things such as silver or gold that you were redeemed from the empty way of life handed down to you from your ancestors, but with the precious blood of Christ, a lamb without blemish or defect. He was chosen before the creation of the world, but was revealed in these last times for your sake. Through him you believe in God, who raised him from the dead and glorified him, and so your faith and hope are in God.

Now that you have purified yourselves by obeying the truth so that you have sincere love for each other, love one another deeply, from the heart. For you have been born again, not of perishable seed, but of imperishable, through the living and enduring word of God. For,

"All people are like grass,
 and all their glory is like the flowers of the field;
the grass withers and the flowers fall,
but the word of the Lord endures forever."

And this is the word that was preached to you.

Teaching point one: Being good opens the door to God's blessing in your life.

God's laws apply to everyone evenly across the board, and he established them in such a way that if you obey, you are blessed, but if you disobey you are not blessed. It's that simple.

Did you ever play the "quiet game" when you were in school? In Mrs. Crider's third-grade class, whenever it rained the students would have to stay inside during recess. That was bad enough, but Mrs. Crider's idea of fun was to have us spend a half hour playing the quiet game. The player stood in front of the class and picked the person who was being the quietest. Of course, everyone in the room was equally quiet. So, what did everyone do? They picked their friends. In fact, there was often a group who agreed in advance to only pick each other. So, even though everyone in the class was being equally quiet, one group picked each other in an endless loop, until Mrs. Crider finally got wise to it.

Some people think God's judgment is like the quiet game—two people can do the same thing and God will bless one and not the other. It doesn't work that way, because God doesn't bless according to whim, he blesses

SESSION 2: WHEN I DON'T FEEL LIKE BEING GOOD

according to his laws.

Pretend two people go to a car dealer and look at the same car. The first guy doesn't know the dealer, and he asks, "How many miles will I get to the gallon?"

The dealer says, "According to the tests that have been done on this car, you'll average 30 miles to the gallon."

The next guy comes to look at the car. He's a friend of the car dealer—an old school chum. (They used to play the quiet game together.) He asks the dealer, "How many miles to the gallon?" and the dealer says, "Well, according to the tests you're supposed to get 30 MPG, but since you're my good friend I'll let you get 40 miles to the gallon." A car dealer can't do that. He can't override the laws of physics and combustion engine design just to do a favor for a friend.

In the same way, God doesn't overlook his laws to give you a special deal on obedience. God judges each man's work impartially. This, according to what you do, will either work for or against you.

There are certain cause-and-effect laws at work in our lives. If you eat right and exercise, you will be healthier than if you eat junk and sit on the couch all day. If you study, you'll make better grades than if you watch TV all day. If you show love and mercy to the people in your life, your relationships will be more rewarding than if you show hostility and judgment. If you obey God, your life will be blessed more than if you disobey. The apostle Paul, who suffered greatly for his faith, agreed with this. Read Romans 2:6–7.

This doesn't mean that everything will be perfect if we obey God, but we will open the door to his blessings.

An electrician said, "I have a healthy respect for electricity, which is to say I'm afraid of what it can do." He isn't afraid to work with or benefit from electricity, but he has a reverent fear of its power. He knows electricity doesn't play favorites. It doesn't matter if you are a master or a novice, if you break the rules, you'll get the shock of your life.

It works the same way with God's laws. Obey and you will be blessed;

disobey and you won't be blessed. If you don't feel like doing good, if you need a motivation for being obedient, this is one reason being good makes sense: It opens the door to God's blessing in your life.

[Q] Does God's blessing mean that everything will go well for us if we obey him? How might the apostles, who died for their faith, answer that question?

Teaching point two: Being good is the right response to the goodness of God.

Walking in obedience and living with integrity is the goal of every believer, but it is not your good works that save your soul. You can't get right with God and earn eternal life by doing good works.

The Bible says that the only way to get right with God is to put our faith in Jesus alone, because Jesus has done everything to bring us into a right relationship with God—at a great price.

If you live a perfect life and never commit a sin—never tell a lie, cheat, steal, think an impure thought, or break any of God's laws—then you, by your own goodness, will be in a right relationship with God. Now, by a show of hands, how many of us qualify? Anyone? I guess not. We all have this in common: we have all sinned.

A father overheard his three sons talking loudly. One boy said, "Oh yeah?

SESSION 2: WHEN I DON'T FEEL LIKE BEING GOOD

Well one day I climbed on top of the house and jumped off and landed on a purple butterfly, and I flew on his back all across town."

And the next boy said, "Oh yeah? Well one day Spot dug a hole in the back yard and when I looked in I could see all the way to China."

And the next boy said, "Oh yeah...."

At this point the father said, "What's going on here? What's all the shouting?"

His oldest son said, "We found a quarter and we don't know whose it is. So we're having a contest. Whoever tells the biggest lie gets to keep it."

The father shook his head and said, "Boys, boys, boys. Where did I go wrong? When I was your age I always shared with my brothers, and I never made a game out of lying."

The boys hung their heads, and the one with the quarter held it out and said, "That's a good one, Dad. I guess you win the quarter."

We have all sinned, the Bible says, and fallen short of God's ideal. No one has lived a perfect life, and we deserve judgment. Each of us must deal with the sin that separates us from God.

The good news is that Jesus dealt with our sin for us. When he died on the cross, his death paid the price for our sins and the punishment we deserve. Every one of us has done things we regret. We would have had to live with the guilt of our actions forever—but Jesus made it possible to be forgiven and be right with God. When we put our faith in him, he forgives us and cleanses us from every bad thing we have done. When we put our faith in him, we are right with him, once and for all, forever and ever.

So, live a life of integrity, not so that God will accept you, but because God has already accepted you. He has forgiven you. When you accept Jesus Christ into your life and allow him to take control, he wipes the slate clean and removes all your guilt and shame. Whatever eternal punishment you deserved, he cancels the debt. In Romans 3 the Living Bible says he acquits you and declares you not guilty.

If you need a reason to be good when you've got a choice to do right or wrong, remember what Jesus did for you. He died on the cross and shed his blood so that you can be forgiven. The only right response to his mercy is to live a life of obedience.

[Q] Which of the following do you think best represents 1 Peter 1:18–21?
a. Since Jesus died for me, I feel guilty and should serve him to pay him back.
b. Since Jesus died for me, I'm convinced of his love for me. Therefore, I want to obey him because he obviously has my best in mind.
c. Since Jesus died for me, I must obey him or I'll be punished.

Why did you pick the statement you did? Which statement would be most motivating to obedience?

Teaching point three: Being good makes you qualified to spread goodness to others.

Peter said, "You purify yourself by obeying the truth," and this enables you to show love to others—a deep and pure love from the heart. The more good you do, the better you become; the better you become, the more you are able to spread goodness to others.

What made it possible for a person like Mother Teresa to do what she did? How could she invest her life ministering to the so-called

SESSION 2: WHEN I DON'T FEEL LIKE BEING GOOD

untouchables of Calcutta, to the poor, to AIDS victims, to the sick and dying? How could she do it? Is it because they are easy to love?

Someone supposedly said to Mother Teresa, "I wouldn't do what you do for a million dollars." Her response was, "Neither would I." Mother Teresa was able to show such love to the unlovely because she was good. She became good through the grace of Jesus Christ, and through her obedience she was able to show more and more love to those who are desperately in need.

Justification happens when you accept Jesus Christ as your savior. Justified means "just-as-if-I'd" never sinned. He wipes the slate clean.

Sanctification means being holy or set apart. This is an ongoing operation in our lives; we are always in the process of becoming holy or good. Peter says you become holy (purified is the word he used) by obeying the truth. You become good by doing good. As you grow in purity, you grow in your ability to show love to others.

In a split-second moment of decision, when you're faced with the temptation to commit a sin, you'll hear a voice saying, "It doesn't matter. No one will know. You can get away with it one more time."

There's another voice, spoken from the pages of Scripture, that says, "If you obey the truth, you will purify yourself and become more holy. And as you become more holy, you will be able to love others more and more and share that love with the world."

When you face the split-second moment of decision, here's the reason to choose good: You need it, and the world needs it. Your obedience makes you a better person and ultimately helps you make the world a better place.

So losing your temper isn't quite so insignificant; making a snide remark isn't quite so harmless; bending the rules isn't quite so inconsequential.

Every time you obey God, it increases your capacity to love others. Being good makes sense because you need it and the world needs it.

[Q] How does obedience to God make us more loving to others?

PART 3
Apply Your Findings

If there are times when you don't feel like being good, welcome to the club. We all have days when we do not live up to what we know we should do. Regardless of how we feel, being good makes sense because when you obey God you open the door to his blessings in your life; when you obey God you express gratitude to him for his love and mercy; and when you obey God you make yourself a better person and, ultimately, the world a better place. If you don't feel like obeying, remember these reasons why being good makes sense.

[Q] What keeps you from obeying God? What is one thing you can do this week to begin overcoming those obstacles?

SESSION 3: AN APPETITE FOR BEING GOOD

An Appetite for Being Good

Mastering the Christian life is like mastering other things: it's a matter of doing the basics again and again.

The apostle Peter told us to "crave pure spiritual milk." Peter wasn't writing these words to new believers only; his letter was written to all kinds of Christians at every imaginable level of maturity. No matter how long you have been a believer, the only way to grow in your salvation—to become spiritual and master the art of obedience—is through pure spiritual milk.

This study will examine four basic elements that contribute to your spiritual growth. If you will make these things part of your daily life, you will develop an appetite for obedience.

Scripture:
1 Peter 2:1–12

Based on:
The sermon "An Appetite for Being Good" by Steve May, *Preaching Today*

SESSION 3: AN APPETITE FOR BEING GOOD

PART 1
Identify the Current Issue

When a baby is born, all the nutrition that baby needs is found in mother's milk. The child grows and develops as it should exclusively on a diet of mother's milk for several months. But eventually there comes a time when the child has to move on to other things, such as strained vegetables. Then, of course, it isn't long before they're eating mashed potatoes, corn, hotdogs, Happy Meals, and pizza. Though it lasts only a few months, there is a period of time when a baby can thrive on nothing but a diet of pure milk.

Even though the baby outgrows its need for pure milk, the believer never does.

There are some basic elements of spiritual nurture—Peter refers to them as "pure spiritual milk"—that all baby Christians need to grow spiritually; but even 10, 20, and 30 years later, the Christian needs that "pure spiritual milk." We go deeper by doing the basics again and again.

The martial art called Tai Chi is a practice of mastering seven basic movements. The obstacle to most students' advancement is not that the technique is too difficult, but that it's too simple. They have a hard time believing they can become Tai Chi experts simply by mastering a few simple moves.

Most things that seem complex are this way. For example, many people are intimidated by computers, but the fact is most computer problems are easy to solve once you have mastered the basics. Computers may seem obstinate, self-willed, and impossible to manage, but if you know the fundamentals, the advanced stuff comes together rather easily.

A school's computer network had gone down, so they called in a computer technician to fix the problem. He quickly surveyed the situation, shut down the network server, reached his hand behind the computer, then turned the server back on. The problem was fixed. The administrator asked him what he had done. The technician was absolutely honest with her. He said, "I jiggled a cable." He then gave her a bill for $125.

She balked at the amount, saying, "How can you charge $125 when all you did was jiggle a cable?"

He shrugged his shoulder and said, "Because I'm the one who knew which cable to jiggle."

PART 2
Discover the Eternal Principles

Teaching point one: Read the Bible.

"For,
"'All people are like grass,
 and all their glory is like the flowers of the field;
the grass withers and the flowers fall,
but the word of the Lord endures forever.'
"And this is the word that was preached to you" (1 Pet. 1:24–25).

Most people think that good Christians read the Bible. But actually, that's getting the equation backwards. It's really that people who read the Bible become good Christians. The Bible is God's Word to us. It tells us how to live—it challenges, motivates, comforts, encourages, and inspires us. When we read the Bible, we become changed by its influence if, and this is a big if, we read it with a heart that is willing to be taught. We have all known people who seem to know a lot of Bible verses, but they only use them as ammunition against other people. They are missing the point of reading Scripture. We don't read the Bible to find out what's wrong with everyone else; we read it to find out what's wrong with us.

When you read the Bible, read with an attitude that says, "God, what are you saying to me? What do I need to do? What do I need to change about the way I think or act? Is there a sin I need to confess? Is there a promise I need to believe? Is there an action I need to avoid? Is there a

SESSION 3: AN APPETITE FOR BEING GOOD

command I need to obey? Is there an example I need to follow?"

One of the key elements of "pure spiritual milk" is the Word of God, and we will never outgrow our need for its daily input in our lives.

[Q] Which of the following methods of learning God's Word do you enjoy most?
- Simply reading it
- Doing an in-depth study on my own
- Studying it with others
- Listening to a sermon
- Memorizing it

Why did you pick the statement you did? If that's what you enjoy most, how might you incorporate more of that method into your life? How might all those methods work together?

Teaching point two: Declare God's praise.

Read 1 Peter 2:9–10:

> But you are a chosen people, a royal priesthood, a holy nation, God's special possession, that you may declare the praises of him

who called you out of darkness into his wonderful light. Once you were not a people, but now you are the people of God; once you had not received mercy, but now you have received mercy.

As Christians, we come together to worship God every week. We sing songs of praise and offer up our prayers, and this is an important part of living the Christian life. However, the praise and worship that takes place in church should be only a small part of the role that praise takes in your daily life. The Bible challenges us to praise God continually throughout the day.

We are created to praise God every day. The more you praise God, the easier it is to master the art of obedience. There are two ways to declare his praises.

Tell it to God. Say to God the things that you know to be true about him: "God, you are so wonderful. You are full of love and forgiveness and mercy. You are the source of truth and light and all that is good. God, you are faithful to me even when I am unfaithful. You forgive me even though I don't deserve to be forgiven. You answer my prayers even though I sometimes don't answer your call. You are my only hope."

God already knows these things to be true. When you declare God's praises, you're not giving him any new information, boosting his self-esteem, buttering him up, or trying to fool him in any way. Instead, you are strengthening your relationship to him.

The difference between acquaintances and people who are in love is that with an acquaintance you talk about surface-level things such as the weather, sports, and politics. When you are in love with someone, you eventually want to talk to that person about your feelings. And the more you talk to another person about your feelings, the stronger the relationship becomes.

There's an old joke about a couple who had been married a long time and the wife said, "Why don't you ever tell me that you love me?"

The husband said, "Twenty-five years ago when I proposed marriage,

SESSION 3: AN APPETITE FOR BEING GOOD

I told you that I love you. Until I take it back, it's still in effect."

Many people think their relationship with God works the same way. They think, "Certainly God knows how I feel. He knows what is in my heart." Tell him anyway. In fact, God commands us to tell him. When you declare his praise, you strengthen the connection between you and God.

Tell it to others. Declaring God's praise means that we also tell others. If you've ever shared your faith with another person, you probably know some people put up a wall of resistance. They think they're about to be preached to. They're afraid they're about to be dumped with a load of guilt and then be pressured into doing something they're afraid to do.

Let's say you run into an acquaintance, and she says to you, "I've got something to tell you. I've got a vacuum cleaner that you need to buy. Even though I've never been there, I know your house is filthy. Stop what you're doing and write a check right now."

How do you think you would respond in that situation? On the other hand, suppose you ran into an acquaintance who said, "Guess what? I'm taking the afternoon off and going on a picnic with my children because all of my housework is done. You see, I bought a new vacuum cleaner, and it's the best one I have ever seen. It gets the place clean from top to bottom. It cleans the carpet, the wood floors, the tile floors, the drapes, the blinds, and it even cleans the kids. This is the most wonderful vacuum cleaner I have ever had, and even with my paltry income I was able to afford it. I don't know how I got along without it."

God didn't ask you to be a salesman. He asked you to declare his praises. Tell others about how good he is, what he has done for you, how much he means to you. It's easy to talk to others about God when you are really talking to them about God. It's when we slip into the vacuum-cleaner-salesman mode that people start to put up walls. Sharing your faith is much more effective when you emphasize how good God is, rather than how bad they are. That's what it means to declare his praises. As you declare God's praises to him and to others you will discover that your appetite for obedience increases dramatically.

[Q] What kinds of things make you most want to praise God: answers to prayer? Beauty in nature? Understanding a truth? Take a few moments to think about it and explain your answer.

Teaching point three: Identify with God's people.

Look again at 1 Peter 2:9–10. As a believer in Jesus Christ, you are part of the most important group of people on planet earth. We are not better than anyone else, but we have the most important job to do—and we're doing it.

Think of all the hospitals that exist right now in the name of Christ. Think of all the colleges, schools, and daycare centers that operate in the name of Christ. Think of all the homeless shelters, orphanages, nursing homes, and soup kitchens that operate in the name of Christ. Think of all the churches that exist throughout the world today. If all of these were to disappear overnight, life on Earth would become unbearable. If all the good things that are being done in the name of Christ were to stop suddenly, the world would spin into chaos. Christ is the glue that is holding this planet together. Even though the world doesn't recognize it, God's people play a crucial role in society, and you are a part of that. When you align yourself with followers of Christ, you align yourself with people who are precious to God and essential to the well being of the global community.

We belong to a people who are precious to God—people with a vital mission. When you focus your attention on the fact that you are part of

SESSION 3: AN APPETITE FOR BEING GOOD

God's people, a people with a purpose, you will find that your appetite for obedience grows.

[Q] Make a list of all the organizations in your community that you know are there because of Christians. Which ones might you be interested in getting involved in?

Teaching point four: Avoid sinful situations.

Read 1 Peter 2:11–12:

> Dear friends, I urge you, as foreigners and exiles, to abstain from sinful desires, which wage war against your soul. Live such good lives among the pagans that, though they accuse you of doing wrong, they may see your good deeds and glorify God on the day he visits us.

There's an old joke about a guy who goes to the doctor and says, "Doctor, it hurts when I move my arm back and forth like this. What should I do?"

The doctor says, "Stop moving your arm back and forth like that." That's bad medical advice, but it's good spiritual advice. If you find that doing certain things, being with certain people, or putting yourself in a certain environment causes you to sin, then avoid those situations.

Do you remember when you would go into the kitchen while your Mom was cooking supper and ask for a snack? She would say, "No, you'll spoil your appetite." It makes sense; eating a bag of potato chips a half hour before mealtime will make you less hungry when it's time to eat.

In the same way, there are certain things in life that will spoil your appetite for obedience. The best thing you can do is avoid them at all costs. There may be some things you have to eliminate—not because they are sinful in themselves, but because they lead you to sin. If you find that listening to a certain kind of music, watching certain TV programs, or being with certain people tends to provoke you to sin, then avoid them at all costs. Don't spoil your appetite.

[Q] What sinful desires war against your soul? Take a few minutes and write them down. These are for your eyes only. When you are done with your list, write what you think you need to do to minimize those desires.

PART 3
Apply Your Findings

If we are going to get good at being good, we need to find our nurture in pure spiritual milk; we need to excel in the basics. We will never outgrow our need for the fundamentals of the Christian life—reading the Bible, declaring God's praise, identifying with God's people, and avoiding sinful situations. To the extent that we master these four simple principles,

SESSION 3: AN APPETITE FOR BEING GOOD

our appetite for obedience will grow, and we will be able to walk the talk according to the will of God.

[Q] Which of the four principles will you work on this week? What specific actions will you take?

SESSION 4: REFUSE TO GET REVENGE

Refuse to Get Revenge

If you refuse to become consumed with the idea of revenge, and instead become consumed with forgiveness, you will experience the grace of God in a powerful way.

If you've ever been taken advantage of, or if you're secretly harboring thoughts of getting even with someone who has done you wrong, this study will challenge the way you feel about the subject. 1 Peter 2 will help you make the transition from wanting to get even to being willing to forgive. We'll examine three things: Why it's best not to seek revenge; what to do instead of seeking revenge; and how to get your mind off of seeking revenge.

Scripture:
1 Peter 2:19–25

Based on:
The sermon "Refusing to Get Revenge" by Steve May, *Preaching Today*

SESSION 4: REFUSE TO GET REVENGE

PART 1
Identify the Current Issue

In February 1990, the Los Angeles County Bomb Squad received a call about a suspicious pickup truck parked in downtown LA. When they checked it, they discovered 400 pounds of explosives in five 55-gallon drums. Had the bomb been detonated, it would have blown a crater 75 feet wide and 20 feet deep. The man they arrested had a history of setting off explosives in the area, though his previous bombs had been small, and no one had ever been injured. This one would have caused severe damage. Why was he doing it? The bombs were all in or near the IRS building. It turns out this man had a vendetta against the IRS. They owed him money, or so he thought, and he wasn't going to leave them alone until he got every penny of it back. The amount he believed they owed to him? Fourteen dollars.

It's hard to believe the desire for revenge can become so strong that someone would destroy lives—including their own—in the quest for it. But it happens again and again.

When you become consumed with revenge, the particulars of the offense lose significance. It could be $14, or it could be $14 million; it could be that someone cut you off in traffic, or it could be that someone did actual bodily harm to you or to someone you love; it could be that a co-worker made a snide remark, or it could be that a co-worker intentionally sabotaged your career. Regardless of the offense, once you have become consumed with the idea of getting revenge, the focus of your life shifts from being good and doing good to getting even. The desire for revenge can destroy you if you let it.

PART 2
Discover the Eternal Principles

Teaching point one: Refusing to seek revenge pleases God and helps you to identify with and be like Christ.

Read 1 Peter 2:19–22:

> For it is commendable if someone bears up under the pain of unjust suffering because they are conscious of God. But how is it to your credit if you receive a beating for doing wrong and endure it? But if you suffer for doing good and you endure it, this is commendable before God. To this you were called, because Christ suffered for you, leaving you an example, that you should follow in his steps.
>
> "He committed no sin,
>   and no deceit was found in his mouth."

The apostle Peter said that when you experience mistreatment of any kind, you can benefit from the experience if you choose not to get revenge. There are three reasons why it's best not to seek revenge.

Refusing revenge is pleasing to God. Look at 1 Peter 2:19–22. The word translated commendable is *charis* in the Greek, which means *grace*. Peter is saying, "If you refuse to get revenge, you will experience God's favor in a special way." Maybe you think getting even would make you happy, but if you refuse to get even, it will make God happy.

The Bible makes it clear that God despises any of kind of mistreatment toward anyone. However, if you refuse to get even with those who take advantage of you, God is pleased with that attitude.

It helps you identify with Christ. No amount of mistreatment you or I will experience can compare with the supreme injustice experienced by

SESSION 4: REFUSE TO GET REVENGE

Christ. On the human level, he was deceived, betrayed, beaten, mocked, and railroaded into a bogus trial where he was sentenced to death on a trumped-up charge. He had done nothing illegal, and yet he was sentenced to die. On the spiritual level, as he hung on the cross, every sin ever committed by you, me, or anyone else was placed upon him. He suffered the punishment for the sins of the world—and he did it willingly.

Maybe you can't heal people, feed 5,000 people with a small amount of fish and bread, or walk on water, but there is one way that you can be just like Jesus. When you are mistreated by anyone for any reason, you can refuse to get even. By doing that you are following in the steps of Christ (v. 21).

It helps you become good. 1 Peter 3:14 says, "But even if you should suffer for what is right, you are blessed. 'Do not fear their threats; do not be frightened.'" 1 Peter 4:1 says, "Therefore, since Christ suffered in his body, arm yourselves also with the same attitude, because whoever suffers in the body is done with sin."

Enduring temptation is like holding a 10-pound weight over your head. If you're not used to it, the weight can get heavy quickly. Enduring mistreatment is much more difficult than enduring temptation—it's like holding a 25-pound weight over your head. The longer you hold it, the stronger you become; when you put down the 25-pound weight of suffering and pick up the 10-pound weight of temptation, it seems light as a feather in comparison.

Nobody in their right mind would choose to be taken advantage of. In fact, you do everything you can to avoid it. But when it happens, you can benefit from it by pleasing God, identifying with Christ, and letting him use it to mold your character.

[Q] Which of these statements best reflects what it means to not seek revenge?
   a. I won't try to get back at others as long as they treat me right.
   b. I will take, without complaining, anything anyone dishes out to me.

c. I will show grace, mercy, and kindness even to those who don't deserve it.

d. I won't do anything physical to someone who has hurt me, but I'll make them suffer emotionally.

Why did you pick the statement you did? Which is the best statement? Why?

Teaching point two: Instead of seeking revenge, show kindness.

There is a difference between getting revenge and taking the necessary steps to put an end to mistreatment. Refusing to get revenge doesn't mean that you refuse to hold others accountable for their actions—it simply means that you refuse to retaliate.

Read Acts 16:35–40:

> When it was daylight, the magistrates sent their officers to the jailer with the order: 'Release those men. The jailer told Paul, "The magistrates have ordered that you and Silas be released. Now you can leave. Go in peace."
>
> But Paul said to the officers: "They beat us publicly without a trial, even though we are Roman citizens, and threw us into

SESSION 4: REFUSE TO GET REVENGE

prison. And now do they want to get rid of us quietly? No! Let them come themselves and escort us out."

The officers reported this to the magistrates, and when they heard that Paul and Silas were Roman citizens, they were alarmed. They came to appease them and escorted them from the prison, requesting them to leave the city. After Paul and Silas came out of the prison, they went to Lydia's house, where they met with the brothers and sisters and encouraged them. Then they left.

When Paul was in the city of Philippi, the authorities beat him and threw him in jail. The next day they offered to set him free and asked him to "go in peace."

Paul said basically, "Not so fast. They beat us publicly without a trial, and we're Roman citizens. They can't sweep this under the rug."

You don't have to be a floor mat for others to trample on. You can set boundaries for yourself, and when you're mistreated, you can do what is possible to prevent it from happening again—whether that means finding a new job, hiring a new employee, ending a friendship, or moving to a new place. Putting an end to unfair treatment is not getting revenge. Getting revenge is when you try to hurt them as much as (or more than) they hurt you.

Instead of getting revenge, this is what you need to do.

Do not retaliate. Read 1 Peter 2:23: "When they hurled their insults at him, he did not retaliate; when he suffered, he made no threats. Instead, he entrusted himself to him who judges justly." There's no such thing as getting even. You can't balance the scales, and your actions will serve only to extend the conflict.

Read what Jesus taught in Matthew 5:38–48:

You have heard that it was said, 'Eye for eye, and tooth for tooth.'

But I tell you, do not resist an evil person. If anyone slaps you on the right cheek, turn to them the other cheek also. And if anyone wants to sue you and take your shirt, hand over your coat as well. If anyone forces you to go one mile, go with them two miles. Give to the one who asks you, and do not turn away from the one who wants to borrow from you.

You have heard that it was said, 'Love your neighbor and hate your enemy.' But I tell you, love your enemies and pray for those who persecute you, that you may be children of your Father in heaven. He causes his sun to rise on the evil and the good, and sends rain on the righteous and the unrighteous. If you love those who love you, what reward will you get? Are not even the tax collectors doing that? And if you greet only your own people, what are you doing more than others? Do not even pagans do that? Be perfect, therefore, as your heavenly Father is perfect.

Do not talk trash. 1 Peter 2:23 says, "when he suffered, he made no threats." Certain athletes in professional sports keep a constant stream of insults and threats directed toward the players of the other team. At a basketball game, one player told his opponent that he was going to "rip your head from your shoulders and feed it to your kidneys." Now, this was an idle threat. All 12 members of the other team went to the locker room at the end of the game with their heads intact. This player was just saying something to keep things stirred up.

Many times when we are taken advantage of, even if we never do anything to get even, we'll talk about it. Maybe we tell the other person off or badmouth them to everyone we know. Or maybe we have imaginary conversations with the enemy while we're driving down the road—rehearsing all the things we would say if we ever got the chance. The problem is that talking trash never solves the problem; it just keeps things stirred up and prevents forgiveness from taking place.

SESSION 4: REFUSE TO GET REVENGE

Put yourself in God's hands. God is a God of justice. In fact, Isaiah said, "[H]e will not falter or be discouraged till he establishes justice on earth" (Isa. 42:4).

God stated in his Word that he will balance the scales. If you have been taken advantage of, put yourself in God's hands and let him take care of it. He will do it much more fairly than you or I could ever hope to do.

"Do not take revenge, my dear friends, but leave room for God's wrath, for it is written: 'It is mine to avenge; I will repay,' says the Lord" (Rom. 12:19).

Do something kind for the one who has hurt you. Romans 12:20 says, "On the contrary: 'If your enemy is hungry, feed him; if he is thirsty, give him something to drink.

In doing this, you will heap burning coals on his head.'"

If you get revenge on your enemy, you may succeed in knocking him off his feet. However, if you forgive him and return kindness instead, you just might drive him to his knees.

When Jesus was dying on the cross, his response to the ones who were mistreating him was, "Father, forgive them; they do not know what they are doing." Instead of seeking revenge, he offered kindness to his enemies.

When someone mistreats you, see if you can find a quiet, subtle way to show kindness. This is what Jesus did: he didn't retaliate, he didn't make threats, but rather he entrusted himself to God and treated his enemies with kindness.

[Q] Why do we have such a strong desire to get even with someone who wrongs us?

Teaching point three: Instead of seeking revenge, forgive.

How do you get your mind off seeking revenge? If you've been taken advantage of, you know that it often has the power to consume your thoughts day and night. The offending person may have forgotten about the incident long ago, but you find yourself struggling with anger and bitterness. Your resentment doesn't hurt them, and it doesn't help you. In fact, if they really have it in for you, nothing would make them happier than to realize that the whole experience is eating you alive while they're happily going on with their lives.

If you have been taken advantage of, and have decided that it's best not to get revenge because you want to please and trust God and treat your enemies with kindness, then you've taken two important steps toward eliminating the problem once and for all. But how do you get rid of the nagging, painful, angry feelings inside? How do you get rid of the desire to get revenge? One way is to say three words to yourself: "I am forgiven."

You may be thinking, *What in the world are you talking about? I don't need to be forgiven! I didn't do anything wrong! I'm the one who was taken advantage of!* That may be true, but it is only when we come to grips with our own need for forgiveness that we are able to forgive others.

After Peter tells his readers why it's best not to seek revenge, he reminds them that they, the ones who are struggling with mistreatment, have been forgiven by God. 1 Peter 2:24–25 reads, "'He himself bore our sins' in his body on the cross, so that we might die to sins and live for righteousness; 'by his wounds you have been healed.' For 'you were like sheep going astray,' but now you have returned to the Shepherd and Overseer of your souls."

There is a saying that hurt people hurt people. People who focus all their energy on an injustice they have been dealt tend to become consumed with it. Their pain often expresses itself in hostility toward the rest of the world. They become bitter, jaded, non-trusting, and distant.

Instead of focusing on unjust suffering, remind yourself that you,

SESSION 4: REFUSE TO GET REVENGE

too, are in need of God's forgiveness—and he has freely and graciously forgiven you. You cannot control what someone else may have done to you, but you can rejoice in the fact that your own sins have been forgiven and that you have been given a fresh start in life. The more you dwell on God's forgiveness, the easier it will be to forgive others—whether they ask for it or not.

[Q] How have you been healed by Christ's wounds (v. 24)? Give practical examples.

PART 3
Apply Your Findings

Chuck Colson tells the story of visiting Jester II, a wing of a Texas prison, run by his organization Prison Fellowship. It's an 18-month program offering an austere, near-monastic atmosphere for hard-core repeat offenders who are truly interested in transforming their lives. At the graduation ceremony for those who had just finished the course, an inmate approached the podium as his name was called. At that time a tall, stately woman walked up to the front, wrapped her arms around the inmate and declared to everyone, "This young man is my adoptive son."

The room was electrified. Colson says he saw hardened criminals and tough correction officers with tears in their eyes, because they knew who the woman was. Her name was Mrs. Washington, and the inmate she embraced was behind bars for murdering her daughter.

For years, Mrs. Washington had refused to forgive this man and had written many angry letters to the Texas Parole Board urging them to deny parole. But after 15 years of resentment, she felt an overwhelming conviction to forgive the man for his horrible crime.

It can be argued that this man doesn't deserve forgiveness, and that she has every right not to forgive. But once she offered her forgiveness for the unjust suffering she had been subjected to, God began to work miracles.

You may have been taken advantage of, mistreated, used, abused. If you have, please remember that Jesus can understand your pain, because he experienced the pain of mistreatment also. If you refuse to become consumed with the idea of revenge, and instead become consumed with the idea of forgiveness, you will experience the grace of God in a powerful way. By his wounds you will be healed.

[Q] Who do you need to forgive? What step will you take today to move toward forgiveness?

SESSION 5: LEARN TO LIVE IN PEACE

Learn to Live in Peace

By working hard at being at peace with one another, we honor God.

If we're not careful, it's easy to forget the priority that Scripture places on unity. We sometimes get sidetracked with our pet theologies—health and wealth, who will be left behind, how many Isaiahs there were, or any number of secondary issues. Meanwhile, God makes it clear that he wants us to get along—and that doing so is foundational to Christian living.

Scripture:
1 Peter 3:8–17

Based on:
The sermon "How to Improve Your Standard of Living" by Steve May, *Preaching Today*

SESSION 5: LEARN TO LIVE IN PEACE

PART 1
Identify the Current Issue

Peter wrote this letter to Christians who were suffering all kinds of trials—slaves suffering at the hands of abusive masters, citizens suffering persecution by an oppressive government, everyday believers suffering slander and mistreatment from those in their community who were hostile to the Christian faith. The primary theme in this epistle is how to deal with suffering—and yet, in the middle of the book, Peter talks about how to simply get along with each other.

In 1 Peter 3:10, he quotes Psalm 34:12. There is not one among us who doesn't love life and want to see good days. That's why Peter tells us how to get that which we certainly all want: a good life. In these verses he mentions three things that are fundamental to finding happiness in our day-to-day existence. To the extent that you incorporate these principles into your life, your quality of living will improve.

PART 2
Discover the Eternal Principles

Teaching point one: Think about what you say.

Read 1 Peter 3:8–11:

> Finally, all of you, be like-minded, be sympathetic, love one another, be compassionate and humble. Do not repay evil with evil or insult with insult. On the contrary, repay evil with blessing, because to this you were called so that you may inherit a blessing. For,
>
> "Whoever would love life
>   and see good days

> must keep their tongue from evil
> and their lips from deceitful speech.
> They must turn from evil and do good;
> they must seek peace and pursue it."

We forget how important our words are. The average person speaks about 25,000 words per day. That would be about 50 pages in print, which means that every week you speak approximately the equivalent of a John Grisham novel. If all your words were put on paper, each year you would compile a personal library of more than 50 such novels. The act of speaking takes up about one-fifth of your life.

If you spend 20 percent of your life doing something, doesn't it deserve your careful attention? Isn't it worth doing right? Peter showed us how Jesus responded to mistreatment in 1 Peter 2:22–24. Jesus set an example for how to respond to mistreatment—and the example is seen primarily in what he didn't say. No deceit, no insults, no threats. In following his example, Peter said to keep your tongue from evil and your lips from deceit (1 Pet. 3:10).

Most human conflict begins on the verbal level. It's what we say that causes problems at work, in our marriages, among our friends, even at church. Keep your tongue from speaking evil.

"The words of the reckless pierce like swords, but the tongue of the wise brings healing" (Prov. 12:18).

"Those who guard their lips preserve their lives, but those who speak rashly will come to ruin" (Prov. 13:3).

"The tongue has the power of life and death, and those who love it will eat its fruit" (Prov. 18:21).

Think about what you say. Your words carry weight and they come with

SESSION 5: LEARN TO LIVE IN PEACE

consequences. Do you want to improve the quality of your life? Begin today to put this principle into practice. Keep your tongue from speaking evil and your lips from telling lies. The best way to get started in this direction is to practice not saying anything at all. Solomon said, "When words are many, sin is not absent, but he who holds his tongue is wise" (Prov. 10:19).

Think about what you say. Talk less. Practice silence. When you do speak, speak carefully—and look for words that will encourage the hearts of those who hear you. Charles Colton said, "We should have all our communications with men as in the presence of God, and with God as in the presence of men."

[Q] How can we learn to talk less and practice silence? Suggest some practical ways.

Teaching point two: Think about what you do.

Read 1 Peter 3:12–17:

> "For the eyes of the Lord are on the righteous
> and his ears are attentive to their prayer,

but the face of the Lord is against those who do evil.

Who is going to harm you if you are eager to do good? But even if you should suffer for what is right, you are blessed. 'Do not fear their threats; do not be frightened.' But in your hearts revere Christ as Lord. Always be prepared to give an answer to everyone who asks you to give the reason for the hope that you have. But do this with gentleness and respect, keeping a clear conscience, so that those who speak maliciously against your good behavior in Christ may be ashamed of their slander. For it is better, if it is God's will, to suffer for doing good than for doing evil.

Maybe Calvin Coolidge had this passage in mind when he said, "Little progress can be made by merely attempting to repress what is evil; our great hope lies in developing what is good."

We all know that there are dos and don'ts in life that we have to live by, but some people never get past focusing on the don'ts. Some Christians define their faith by what they don't do: I don't drink, smoke, listen to secular music, wear certain types of clothes, let my children watch certain movies, and on and on. And, of course, there are more serious types of evil that we have to turn away from, such as gossip, anger, jealousy, selfish ambition, lust, greed, and so on. But in addition to turning away from doing bad things, we need to also put energy into doing good things.

We need to keep an eye on both, of course. We need to turn away from the evil that always seeks to creep into our lives. And, just as importantly, we need to seek out opportunities to do good. God spoke through the prophet Isaiah: "Wash and make yourselves clean. Take your evil deeds out of my sight; stop doing wrong" (Isa. 1:16). When many people think about having a relationship with God, this is what they think it entails: repent; turn from evil; clean up your life. But Isaiah continues, "Learn to do right; seek justice. Defend the oppressed. Take up the cause of the fatherless; plead the case of the widow" (Isa. 1:17).

SESSION 5: LEARN TO LIVE IN PEACE

Do you want to experience the good life? Make it a daily priority to find opportunities to do good. It's not about keeping score so that you can pat yourself on the back. It is about evaluating your life to ensure that you live by your priorities. Look for chances to do good, and do it.

[Q] Which of the following describes what our motive should be in doing good?
a. To be rewarded in heaven
b. To earn favor with God
c. To earn a place in heaven
d. To show my joy in what God has done for me

Why did you pick the statement you did? How does it motivate you to do good?

Teaching point three: Think about your attitude toward others.

Peter told us to pursue peace (1 Pet. 3:11). It's not easy to live at peace with others, but it's necessary. Read what Paul wrote in Romans 12:17-18 and 14:19:

"Do not repay anyone evil for evil. Be careful to do what is right in the eyes of everyone. If it is possible, as far as it depends on you, live at peace with everyone" (12:17-18).

"Let us therefore make every effort to do what leads to peace and to mutual edification" (14:19).

You probably have a reason to hold a grudge against every person you know. More than likely your spouse has said or done something that you could hold against him or her forever. The same can be said for your co-workers and employer. Everyone has a good reason to hold a grudge against someone. Get over it. Rise above it. Let it go.

Do you want to improve your standard of living? Think about your attitude toward others. Work hard at living in peace with them. In fact, make it your goal to be better at this than anyone else. In your family, at your job, in the church, work harder at getting along than anyone else is willing to work. Be more patient than anyone else is willing to be. Bend more than anyone is willing to bend.

Will this make you a doormat? No, it will make you like Jesus. And God will see what you do. Listen to Peter's words: "[T]he eyes of the Lord are on the righteous and his ears are attentive to their prayers" (1 Pet. 3:12). It's as simple as this: When you make an effort to get along with others, God takes notice.

[Q] Why is God attentive to the prayers of the righteous? What does that mean in practical terms?

SESSION 5: LEARN TO LIVE IN PEACE

PART 3
Apply Your Findings

Philip Bailey said, "The goodness of the heart is shown in deeds of peacefulness and kindness." Our actions reflect our nature. What we do tells the world who we are.

So who are we? We are God's people, who have been saved through the power of his blood and his resurrection. We have experienced his forgiveness, mercy, and acceptance. We have been given eternal life through his Son, Jesus Christ. How can we respond? By treating others as God has treated us.

Think about what you say. Follow the example of Jesus. Be slow to speak; keep silent if necessary.

Think about what you do. Every day look for the chance to do something for someone else.

Think about your attitude toward others, even those who have offended you. Seek to be at peace with everyone. Try harder than anyone else is willing to try.

If you apply these standards to your life, your standard of living will change. According to God's promise, he will take notice.

[Q] How will you start applying these standards today?

SESSION 6: GET READY FOR A ROUGH RIDE

Get Ready for a Rough Ride

Things get rough from time and time, but you can prepare yourself for the difficult days ahead.

The apostle Peter tried to prepare us to live boldly in tough times. He wrote this letter to encourage believers to live a life of courage in spite of the hardships they faced, such as poverty, oppression, persecution, slander, abandonment, and loneliness. This study of 1 Peter 4 will help prepare you in advance for the tough times that surely are ahead.

Scripture:
1 Peter 4:1–19

Based on:
The sermon "Get Ready for a Rough Ride" by Steve May, *Preaching Today*

SESSION 6: GET READY FOR A ROUGH RIDE

PART 1
Identify the Current Issue

From the beginning, Peter makes it clear that we will experience many different kinds of trials. Jesus said that God "sends rain on the righteous and the unrighteous" (Matt. 5:45); everyone goes through hard times. It's inevitable and inescapable. The question is: How will you respond? In 1 Peter 4, Peter prepares us to answer that question. He begins this chapter, "Therefore, since Christ suffered in his body, arm yourselves also with the same attitude" (v. 1). He's saying, "Get ready. Jesus suffered. So will you." Things get rough from time and time—there's no getting around that—but you can prepare yourself for the difficult days ahead. Peter shows us what we need to do to.

PART 2
Discover the Eternal Principles

Read 1 Peter 4:1–19:

> Therefore, since Christ suffered in his body, arm yourselves also with the same attitude, because whoever suffers in the body is done with sin. As a result, they do not live the rest of their earthly lives for evil human desires, but rather for the will of God. For you have spent enough time in the past doing what pagans choose to do—living in debauchery, lust, drunkenness, orgies, carousing and detestable idolatry. They are surprised that you do not join them in their reckless, wild living, and they heap abuse on you. But they will have to give account to him who is ready to judge the living and the dead. For this is the reason the gospel was preached even to those who are now dead, so that they might be judged according to human standards in regard to the body, but live according to God in regard to the spirit. The end of all

things is near. Therefore be alert and of sober mind so that you may pray. Above all, love each other deeply, because love covers over a multitude of sins. Offer hospitality to one another without grumbling. Each of you should use whatever gift you have received to serve others, as faithful stewards of God's grace in its various forms. If anyone speaks, they should do so as one who speaks the very words of God. If anyone serves, they should do so with the strength God provides, so that in all things God may be praised through Jesus Christ. To him be the glory and the power for ever and ever. Amen.

Dear friends, do not be surprised at the fiery ordeal that has come on you to test you, as though something strange were happening to you. But rejoice inasmuch as you participate in the sufferings of Christ, so that you may be overjoyed when his glory is revealed. If you are insulted because of the name of Christ, you are blessed, for the Spirit of glory and of God rests on you. If you suffer, it should not be as a murderer or thief or any other kind of criminal, or even as a meddler. However, if you suffer as a Christian, do not be ashamed, but praise God that you bear that name. For it is time for judgment to begin with God's household; and if it begins with us, what will the outcome be for those who do not obey the gospel of God? And,

"If it is hard for the righteous to be saved,
   what will become of the ungodly and the sinner?"

So then, those who suffer according to God's will should commit themselves to their faithful Creator and continue to do good.

SESSION 6: GET READY FOR A ROUGH RIDE

Teaching point one: Prepare your mind.

In 1 Peter 4:1–6, Peter tells us to arm ourselves with the same attitude Christ had. Some Bible translations use the word "purpose" instead of "attitude." It reminds us that there is a reason for our suffering. As we saw in chapter one, our problems have a point. Your hard times are not just random events that occur in your life. They can serve a purpose—if you allow them to.

Peter wrote, "[W]hoever suffers in the body is done with sin" (1 Pet. 4:1). He's not talking about sinless perfection, but the strength to endure suffering, which causes temptation to lose its power in your life. When you have endured suffering, you become aware of just how much power you have in Christ, and of how little power Satan has over you.

The tendency to give in to temptation is often based on the misconception that the sin is stronger than you are. We think, *I can't control my temper. Why try? I can't love the unlovable. Why try? I can't say no to pizza. Why try?* However, the more you suffer, the more you make it through hard times, the easier it is to say no to temptation. Enduring suffering gives you a sense of fearlessness and confidence—not in yourself, but in God's power at work in your life.

Philippians 4:13 says, "I can do all this through him who gives me strength." For some of us, these words are a proclamation of faith. For others, as it was with Paul, these words are a proclamation of testimony. Paul wasn't merely talking about the future; he was mostly talking about the past. He was saying, in effect, "I have been through good times and bad, and I know from experience that I can do all things through Christ. This is my testimony, and because of this, I face the future with confidence."

When you endure suffering, it can become your testimony too. The more you endure, the more you understand how powerful God's presence is in your life. Peter said, "Prepare your mind for suffering, because this gives you power over sin."

Read 1 Peter 4:12–13 again. Everyone goes through hard times. In certain areas and during certain generations, some Christians suffer more than others, but we all suffer to some extent. American Christians tend to think that our money and freedom exempts us from tough times. But how many of you have already learned that tough times are about more than financial hardship and political oppression?

Many of us say, "How could this happen to me? How could a loving God allow this in my life? Doesn't he want me to be happy? What did I do to deserve this?" Tough times are able to blindside us, because we think that we should be exempt from suffering. But no Christian has such an exemption.

[Q] Why do you think Peter told us to "arm" ourselves with an attitude like Christ's? How can we do that?

Teaching point two: Prepare your soul.

1 Peter 4: 7 reminds us to pray. Here is a powerful two-step approach for improving your prayer life. First, take it seriously. Realize that when you talk to God, you are talking to the Creator of the universe. Stop for a moment and think about what an incredible privilege that is. Have you ever had a brush with greatness? Ever had the chance to speak to someone famous or powerful? It's an amazing feeling. Well, each and every day we have a chance for a brush with greatness: Our great God will listen to our prayers. How can it be, then, that we so often avoid praying or simply go through the motions? We need to remind ourselves of the

SESSION 6: GET READY FOR A ROUGH RIDE

awesome privilege that prayer is.

Number two in this two-step approach is to discipline yourself. Whether your prayers are effective or not might depend on your consistency. Do you want to become effective in your prayer life? Discipline yourself to do it daily. You will find that the more you pray on a daily basis, the more strength you will have to face whatever life brings you.

To prepare your soul, you have to be willing to take a long, hard look at yourself. You cannot endure hard times unless you are willing to get your eyes off everyone else and focus on your own life. Peter said, "For it is time for judgment to begin with God's household" (v. 17). When Bob Dylan began writing protest songs in the '60s, he called them his "finger-pointing songs." These were songs in which he blasted the establishment for everything that was wrong with it. Some Christians think this is what we are supposed to do, too: that we're to criticize all that is wrong in the world and tell everyone about every bad thing they do. Some people think if a preacher doesn't talk about how awful things are, they haven't heard a sermon.

But usually when people ask, "Why don't you preach against sin?" they don't mean their own sin. Many people don't want to be challenged to face their own sin. They just want to hear about how wicked the rest of the world is.

But Peter says, "It is time for judgment to begin with the household of God." This doesn't mean that we move from criticizing the world to criticizing the church. That's missing the point. We need to take a long hard look at ourselves. It is time for judgment to begin in the house of God, and each member of the household is responsible to God.

If your Christian life consists primarily of taking notice of what everyone else is doing wrong, you will not be ready when the rough ride begins. Prepare your soul. Get serious about prayer and take a long hard look at your spiritual life.

[Q] What do you spend most of your time praying about?
   a. Forgiveness of sins
   b. Strength to serve
   c. Praise to God
   d. Asking for things
   e. Praying for others
   f. Wisdom and guidance

Why did you pick the statement you did? What do you think you should spend most of your time praying about? Why?

Teaching point three: Prepare your heart.

Read 1 Peter 4:8 again. "Love covers over a multitude of sins": Whose sins is Peter talking about? He's not talking about our sins and guilt before a holy God. He's talking about our sins and how they affect our relationships with other believers. It works both ways. When you love someone, you tend to overlook their sins, and they tend to overlook yours.

The Christian life is not about finger-pointing. It's about mercy and compassion, tolerance and acceptance. It pleases God for us to get along. If you have children, you know what a delight it is when they get along. This is how God feels about us.

Psalm 133:1 says, "How good and pleasant it is when God's people live together in unity!" If you want to be ready for tough times, begin today

SESSION 6: GET READY FOR A ROUGH RIDE

to practice the habit of loving others. How? Peter is very practical on this point. He tells us to:

- **Accommodate others.** 1 Peter 4:9 says, "Offer hospitality to one another without grumbling." What can you do to make others feel more welcome? This is a question every church body—as well as every believer—should ask. How can we be hospitable? How can we make our guests feel more at home? How can we share our resources with others?

- **Serve one another.** 1 Peter 4:10 says, "Each of you should use whatever gift you have received to serve others, as faithful stewards of God's grace in its various forms." You were given certain skills, abilities, and gifts to help people. If what you have and what you do doesn't benefit others, you are wasting your resources. Look for opportunities to put your gifts to work.

- **Encourage one another.** 1 Peter 4:11 says, "If anyone speaks, they should do so as one who speaks the very words of God." As he has so many times throughout this letter, Peter comes back to the subject of how we use our words. He challenges us to speak the very words of God. Here's the challenge: In speaking to one another, we need to get into the habit of saying that which we believe Jesus would say, and of not saying that which Jesus wouldn't say. Learn to speak, as it were, the very words of God.

If you've played sports on both united and divided teams, you undoubtedly know the difference between playing on winning and losing teams. It is difficult, if not impossible, for a divided team to win consistently. That's why Peter tells us that if the church expects to endure hardship, we must be unified. We need to be committed to one another, doing all that we can to live peacefully together.

It's a matter of the heart. Prepare your heart to love, serve, and minister to others. Doing this prepares you for whatever life brings your way.

[Q] What do you think it means to "love each other deeply" (v. 8)? What are some practical ways we can do that?

PART 3
Apply Your Findings

Suffering is inevitable and unavoidable. We must do what we can to prepare. This means that we need to prepare our minds by seeing suffering for what it can accomplish in our lives: "Whoever suffers in the body is done with sin." We need to prepare our souls by getting serious about prayer and taking a long, hard look at our spiritual lives. And we need to prepare our hearts by serving one another in love.

You could say it this way: We need to stop judging others and start judging ourselves, and we need to stop serving ourselves and start serving others.

[Q] This week, what are the steps you'll take to stop judging others and serve them instead?

SESSION 7: YOU'RE IN GOOD HANDS

You're in Good Hands

You are in God's hands.

We will face hard times, but God promises to make it worth our while. Whatever difficulties this life holds, faithfulness and obedience to God will be rewarded beyond what the hardship costs us. This study looks at why we can trust God with it all.

Scripture:
1 Peter 5:5–11

Based on:
The sermon "You're in Good Hands" by Steve May, *Preaching Today*

SESSION 7: YOU'RE IN GOOD HANDS

PART 1
Identify the Current Issue

Have you ever noticed that the fear of getting a shot is often worse than the shot itself? You dread the moment—then it happens, and you discover that you got through it just fine and wonder why you wasted so much time worrying about it.

It's often the same way with hard times. We wonder, *What will I do if such and such happens? How will I get by? How will I survive?* Then it happens, and we discover that we can get through it. It doesn't mean we like it or that it's easy, but we can get through it.

As sure as the sun will rise tomorrow, you will face tough times. It's inevitable, unavoidable, and inescapable. Sooner or later, if not right now, you will be up against some health, money, job, family, or marriage problems. There may be people who oppose you for no reason other than they decide to bring trouble into your life. Or you may find yourself being punished for trying to do good.

A couple of teenage girls from Colorado learned this lesson. Instead of going to a weekend party where there might be drinking, they decided to stay home and make cookies for their rural neighbors. They dressed the cookies with little pink hearts and wrote a note that said, "Have a great night." They rang the doorbell of each home and left the cookies on the doorstep. Sounds like your basic, run-of-the-mill good deed. However, one of their neighbors didn't appreciate their thoughtfulness. She later filed a lawsuit against the girls, claiming that the unsolicited cookies triggered an anxiety attack that forced her to go to the hospital. Amazingly, the judge ordered the girls to pay over $900 in medical bills and court costs. That's more than $450 each, probably a month's pay for the typical teenager with a part-time job. Can you believe that one simple act of kindness could backfire in such a way?

There will be times when the events in your life take an unexpected and unpleasant turn, and you will find yourself exactly where you don't want to be. Don't waste time worrying over something you can certainly get through. The phrase "you can certainly get through" is our trump card. We have an advantage nonbelievers don't: We have God's promise to see us through whatever storms life brings our way. Peter closes his letter to suffering Christians with an encouraging word: "You're in good hands," he says, "because you're in God's hands, and he will not let you go."

PART 2
Discover the Eternal Principles

Read 1 Peter 5:5–11:

> In the same way, you who are younger, submit yourselves to your elders. All of you, clothe yourselves with humility toward one another, because,
>
> "God opposes the proud
>   but shows favor to the humble."
>
> Humble yourselves, therefore, under God's mighty hand, that he may lift you up in due time. Cast all your anxiety on him because he cares for you.
>
> Be alert and of sober mind. Your enemy the devil prowls around like a roaring lion looking for someone to devour. Resist him, standing firm in the faith, because you know that the family of believers throughout the world is undergoing the same kind of sufferings.
>
> And the God of all grace, who called you to his eternal glory in Christ, after you have suffered a little while, will himself restore you and make you strong, firm and steadfast. To him be the power

SESSION 7: YOU'RE IN GOOD HANDS

for ever and ever. Amen.

Teaching point one: God will honor you if you humble yourself.

Verse six says that if we humble ourselves under God's mighty hand, he will lift us up. This means that God will give you the credit, recognition, esteem, and appreciation you deserve. Since God has promised to do this, you don't have to do it yourself. This should be a tremendous relief for all of us. We don't have to do our own PR. God will handle it for us.

Don King once said, "I am the greatest boxing promoter in the world. And, of course, I say that humbly." True? Maybe. Humble? No. Will Rogers said, "Get someone else to toot your horn, and the sound will carry twice as far." Allow God to honor you, and you won't have to worry about honoring yourself. He will take care of it, but it will happen according to his timetable, not yours. If it isn't happening now, it's because—in his wisdom—he knows that it is better for you and for his kingdom that you be given honor then instead of now. But at the proper time, he will exalt you. It may not be until we reach heaven, but we will be rewarded

The phrase "God's mighty hand" can be disconcerting. Many of us interpret that to be a stern phrase, as if it actually said, "God's mighty fist." That's not what it means. In Scripture, the phrase "the hand of God" symbolizes the deliverance of God. Exodus 13:9 says, "This observance will be for you like a sign on your hand and a reminder on your forehead that this law of the Lord is to be on your lips. For the Lord brought you out of Egypt with his mighty hand."

We are to humble ourselves under his mighty hand. Three characteristics of being humble are:

- Being aware of where the power comes from. It's God's power, not yours.

- Being willing to do good without getting credit for it.

- Being able to rejoice in someone else's success.

Work on being humble. God will exalt you at the proper time.

[Q] How can you tell whether you are being humble?

Teaching point two: God will take care of you.

Caring, by the way, is not an emotion. It's an action. God takes care of you, like a parent takes care of a child. He knows what you need and when you need it.

Sometimes we think we have a financial need, but what we really need is to learn to live on less. Sometimes we think we need companionship, but what we really need is to develop intimacy in our relationship to Christ. Sometimes we think we need healing, but what we really need is to learn compassion and mercy for those who are suffering. Many times we think we need this when, in reality, we need that. The great thing about knowing Jesus is that when we need that, he gives us that! He takes care of us. He gives us what we really need.

What's our responsibility? Peter used the word "cast." It means to throw. Intellectually, toss your worries as far away from your mind as you can. Drop them into the sea of God's mercy and tender loving care. One by one, as anxieties present themselves to you, you need to make a spiritual decision to cast them as far as you can in God's direction. He

SESSION 7: YOU'RE IN GOOD HANDS

will take care of them for you, because he has promised.

[Q] Which of the following best describes worry?
 a. Lack of faith in God
 b. Reasonable response to the stress of life
 c. Necessary to be prepared for life
 d. Unavoidable since we're human

Why did you pick the statement you did? How does that attitude affect your life?

Teaching point three: God will restore you.

Have you ever made a bad investment? You buy, for example, $1,000 in stocks, and a few days later they're worth $600. All you can think about is how nice it would be to have the $400 back. One of the most difficult aspects of suffering is the ground you lose in the process. Many times our problems not only slow us down; they knock us back a few paces. Soon we discover we're just not where we used to be in life. It's hard not to look at what we have lost. It's hard not to think about where we would be and what we would have if things had turned out differently. Our mantra becomes, "If only ... If only ... If only ..." The longer we look at what we have lost, the stronger the grip of regret becomes on our life. It can consume us.

The truth is that everyone loses ground from time to time. We all have setbacks. We all find ourselves back at the starting gate sometimes. But God has made a promise to his people: these setbacks are temporary. Reread 1 Peter 5:10–11. What a promise!

- God will restore you. He will put you back where you belong.
- He will support you. The original Greek word means "to make as solid as a rock."
- He will strengthen you. This is an athletic term. Peter is saying, "God will give you the muscle to do what you need to do."
- He will place you on a firm foundation. He'll put your feet on solid ground.
- No matter what you're going through right now, this is what God has in mind for your future.

What's your part in this? Read 1 Peter 5:8–9 again. Satan is like a roaring lion looking for someone to devour. So "stand up," Peter says. "Stand against him. Don't let yourself be pushed around by ungodly circumstances in your life. Be strong in your faith." Being strong is within your ability. He isn't telling you to do something beyond your ability. You can do it. It comes down to a choice, a decision, a determination. Be strong. Take a stand. God will restore you, support you, strengthen you, and place you on a solid foundation.

[Q] What does Peter mean when he tells us to be self-controlled and alert (v. 8)? What would that look like in your life?

PART 3
Apply Your Findings

Peter closes this letter with this idea: "I have written to you briefly,

SESSION 7: YOU'RE IN GOOD HANDS

encouraging you and testifying that this is the true grace of God. Stand fast in it" (v. 12). Just before this he says, "[Y]ou know that the family of believers throughout the world is undergoing the same kind of sufferings" (v. 9). When you face hard times—and all of us certainly will—it is easy to think, I am all alone in this; there is no one to stand with me. Remember, you are not alone. And no matter what happens, God's grace is with you. You can endure anything life has to give. You are in good hands. He will honor you. He will take care of you. He will restore your life.

[Q] How will you remember that this week? How will you take these promises to heart?

Discussion Guide

Leader's note: In this guide, we've included questions for each study (including those already featured in the studies). Feel free to pick and choose a few discussion starters that make the most sense for your group.

SESSION 1: THE BATTLE FOR HOLINESS

PART 1
Identify the Current Issue

Discussion starters:
[Q] What comes to your mind when you hear the word holy? Why do you think that is your perception?

[Q] Does it seem impossible to be holy? Why or why not?

[Q] Describe the life of someone you consider to be a holy person. What makes them holy?

PART 2
Discover the Eternal Principles
Teaching point one: To be holy, you must prepare your mind for action.

[Q] What are some practical ways we can prepare our minds for holiness?

Leader's Note: Some possible answers are Scripture, prayer, uplifting music, good books, sermons, and edifying conversation.

[Q] Look again at verse 13. What does self-control have to do with being holy?

[Q] What might you need to say no to in order to prepare your mind for holiness?

[Q] According to verse 13, what has God given us to help us be holy? Why would that help?

Optional Activity

Purpose: To help us learn what it means to be holy.
Activity: The following people want to prepare their minds to be holy. How would you advise them? Split your group up into three smaller groups and have each brainstorm practical ways that one of these three people might begin to change their routines and lifestyles.

- Shannon spends at least three hours a day watching TV. What might she do to break this habit and replace it with better things?
- Cornelius spends every waking minute with people. He can't stand to be alone. How might he learn to face alone time so that he can learn to listen to God?
- Frank uses alcohol to numb the guilt he constantly feels. How can he find relief from guilt so that he can depend on God instead of alcohol?

Teaching point two: To be holy, you must think differently.

[Q] Which of the following best describes a holy life?
   a. Never indulging in anything pleasurable
   b. Never sinning
   c. Only thinking about spiritual things
   d. Being passionately in love with Christ, which colors the way you think and act

Why did you pick the statement you did? How does it affect the way you view holiness? What would be the difference between d. and the other choices? What is wrong with choices a.–c.?

Leader's Note: a. God created pleasure and delights in our enjoyment of the good gifts he has given us, as long as our pleasure doesn't lead us to sin. b. Although we should avoid sin, we will still sin and need to ask

SESSION 1: THE BATTLE FOR HOLINESS

forgiveness. c. Although we should be consumed with pleasing God, we will necessarily have to think of earthly things to survive. d. As we fall in love with Christ, we will naturally want to please him. Love is a far greater motivator than fear.

[Q] Peter compares us to obedient children. Why would we want to be such?

[Q] What are the evil desires Peter mentions in verse 14? What does it mean to conform to those desires?

[Q] Why were we in ignorance before? What brought us out of ignorance?

[Q] What do you think it means "to be holy in all you do"?

[Q] How can you learn to separate your thoughts from your emotions? Give practical examples.

Teaching point three: To be holy, you must learn to concentrate on God rather than your own efforts.

[Q] Why must we have God's grace to live a holy life? Why are our own efforts doomed to fail?

Leader's Note: We need God's power, strength, and mercy to live a holy life. Our own efforts are as weak as we are.

[Q] How can we learn to depend on God's grace, rather than our own efforts?

Leader's Note: By admitting our inadequacy and asking God for power. For example, if you cannot love someone, admit it to God. Ask him to love that person through you.

[Q] How is the example of the little girl running to the base similar to how we should focus on Jesus?

Leader's Note: We should be running toward Christ with all our might, without being distracted by the world around us.

[Q] Why do you think God said, "Be holy, because I am holy"? How can we obey that without becoming discouraged? Does he mean that we have to be as perfect as he is? If not, what does he mean?

Leader's Note: He knows we can never be perfect. Instead he wants us to do what we've covered in this study—prepare our minds, think differently, and concentrate on him.

[Q] Read 1 Peter 1:1–16. Peter spent much of the chapter talking about hope. How does this help you in your effort to live a holy life? Name as many encouragements as you see in this passage.

PART 3
Apply Your Findings

Action Point: Ask the group if this study changed any of their ideas about holiness. If so, what do they most need to rethink? Pray together for each individual that God will retrain each person's thinking.

SESSION 2: WHEN I DON'T FEEL LIKE BEING GOOD

PART 1
Identify the Current Issue

Discussion starters:
[Q] How would you define "being good"?

[Q] What is the hardest part about being good?

[Q] What causes us to fail to want to be good?

PART 2
Discover the Eternal Principles
Teaching point one: Being good opens the door to God's blessing in your life.

[Q] Does God's blessing mean that everything will go well for us if we obey him? How might the apostles, who died for their faith, answer that question?

Leader's Note: The apostles certainly felt blessed because God was using them in a powerful way. They also felt blessed because they were no longer enslaved to sin, but living purposeful lives. Blessing does not mean we won't have problems; we just have purpose and direction in the midst of them.

[Q] What does it mean that God judges each person's work impartially?

[Q] What does it mean to have a reverent fear of God?

Leader's Note: We should fear God when we thumb our nose at him in disobedience, not when we are trying to do what is right. He is a just and loving God, but he is also powerful and holds our eternal future.

[Q] How are God's impartiality and our reverent fear of him different from our relationships with our earthly fathers?

Teaching point two: Being good is the right response to the goodness of God.

[Q] Which of the following do you think best represents 1 Peter 1:18–21?
 a. Since Jesus died for me, I feel guilty and should serve him to pay him back.
 b. Since Jesus died for me, I'm convinced of his love for me. Therefore, I want to obey him because he obviously has my best in mind.
 c. Since Jesus died for me, I must obey him or I'll be punished.

Why did you pick the statement you did? Which statement would be most motivating to obedience?

[Q] What kind of empty way of life was handed down by our forefathers?

[Q] How does knowing that Christ shed his blood for you motivate you to obey God? What does that tell you about God? Name as many things as you can think of.

[Q] Why does the fact that God raised Christ from the dead (v. 21) motivate us to obedience?

[Q] How do our faith and hope (v. 21) also motivate us to obedience?

[Q] Give human examples of how someone's love and commitment to you motivated you to be a better person. How might this compare to God's love and commitment to us?

SESSION 2: WHEN I DON'T FEEL LIKE BEING GOOD

Teaching point three: Being good makes you qualified to spread goodness to others.

[Q] How does obedience to God make us more loving to others?

[Q] If our so-called obedience is not making us more loving to others, what should that tell us? Give examples of things that might look like obedience, but in fact make a person less loving.

[Q] What does it mean to love deeply from the heart (v. 22)?

[Q] Why does the frailty of humans (v. 24) make it even more important that we love others?

[Q] In what way is God's Word the key to obedience (v. 25)?

PART 3
Apply Your Findings

Action Point: Ask each person in the group to list the reasons why they often do not want to obey God. Then ask them to look over the teaching points again and write next to their reasons what they can do to counteract those feelings. Close in prayer asking God for the courage to choose what is right in the day-to-day decisions we make.

Optional Activity

Purpose: To help us soak in the fact that God loves us more than we can imagine.
Activity: Using a concordance, take time this week to look up every verse you can find on God's love for you, and write them down. Share your findings with the group next week.

SESSION 3: AN APPETITE FOR BEING GOOD

PART 1
Identify the Current Issue

Discussion starters:
[Q] What do you think is the pure spiritual milk Peter refers to in 1 Peter 2:2?

[Q] What do you think it means to grow up in your salvation?

[Q] What things have caused you to grow the most in your faith so far?

PART 2
Discover the Eternal Principles
Teaching point one: Read the Bible.

[Q] Which of the following methods of learning God's Word do you enjoy most?
- Simply reading it
- Doing an in-depth study on my own
- Studying it with others
- Listening to a sermon
- Memorizing it

Why did you pick the statement you did? If that's what you enjoy most, how might you incorporate more of that method into your life? How might all those methods work together?

[Q] Why does the Word of the Lord stand forever?

[Q] What does that tell us about our need for it?

[Q] How does our love for God's Word reflect our love (or lack of love) for him?

[Q] What hinders you from regularly reading God's Word? How might you get past those hindrances?

Teaching point two: Declare God's praise.

[Q] What kinds of things make you most want to praise God: Answers to prayer? Beauty in nature? Understanding a truth? Take a few moments to think about it and explain your answer to the group.

[Q] Name some of the reasons we can praise God according to these verses.

[Q] What kinds of darkness did God call you out of?

Optional Activity

Purpose: To help us practice praising God to others.
Activity: In pairs, take turns declaring God's praises to each other. It can be for specific things God has done recently, general things he has done over the long haul, or simply praising him for who he is.

Teaching point three: Identify with God's people.

[Q] Make a list of all the organizations in your community that you know are there because of Christians.

[Q] What does it mean that we are a chosen people (v. 9)? That we are a royal priesthood? A holy nation?

Leader's Note: We are chosen to be God's children in Christ. We are all made priests because we've been given the job of reconciling others to Christ. We are a holy nation, because the body of Christ supersedes all earthly nations.

SESSION 3: AN APPETITE FOR BEING GOOD

[Q] How can we declare God's praises as a group? List as many ways as you can think of.

[Q] How can we let the world around us know that God has shown us mercy (v. 10)?

Teaching point four: Avoid sinful situations.

[Q] What sinful desires war against your soul? Take a few minutes and write them down. These are for your eyes only. When you are done with your list, write what you think you need to do to minimize those desires.

[Q] Why should we look at ourselves as aliens and strangers in the world (v. 11)? How can that help us in our obedience to Christ?

[Q] How might your good deeds cause someone else to glorify God (v. 12)?

PART 3
Apply Your Findings

Action Point: Close the group in silent prayer. Ask each group member to pray about the things they need to change, listed after the second question under Teaching Point Four.

SESSION 4: REFUSE TO GET REVENGE

PART 1
Identify the Current Issue

Discussion starter:
[Q] Ask the individuals in your group to briefly describe a book or movie that shows the consequences of seeking revenge. Describe one that shows the freedom of forgiving instead of seeking revenge.

PART 2
Discover the Eternal Principles
Teaching point one: Refusing to seek revenge pleases God and helps you to identify with and be like Christ.

[Q] Which of these statements best reflects what it means to not seek revenge?
  a. I won't try to get back at others as long as they treat me right.
  b. I will take, without complaining, anything anyone dishes out to me.
  c. I will show grace, mercy, and kindness even to those who don't deserve it.
  d. I won't do anything physical to someone who has hurt me, but I'll make them suffer emotionally.

Why did you pick the statement you did? Which is the best statement? Why?

[Q] Why is it commendable if we bear up under the pain of unjust suffering (v. 19)? What would our attitude need to be like for this to be commendable?

Leader's Note: If we bear up under it with a bitter attitude, it cannot please God. If we have an attitude like Christ's, it is commendable—the last part of verse 19 says "because he is conscious of God."

[Q] Have you ever had to suffer unjustly? What happened? How could you have a commendable attitude through that experience?

[Q] Why should we expect to suffer unjustly (v. 21)?

[Q] What do you think it means to follow in his steps (v. 21)?

[Q] What do these verses say about the American idea that we should fight for our rights?

Teaching point two: Instead of seeking revenge, show kindness.

[Q] How can you learn to put yourself in God's hands instead of seeking revenge on your own? Suggest practical ways.

[Q] Why do we have such a strong desire to get even with someone who wrongs us?

[Q] Why is talking badly about the one who wronged us so satisfying? When is it valid to talk about the person and when does it cross over into sin?

Leader's Note: Sometimes we will need to talk about it with a mature Christian to process it and gain understanding. It turns into sin when we just want to hurt the other person.

[Q] How can you change your attitude enough to do something kind for the one who hurt you? Has anyone ever done this for you? If so, how did it make you feel?

SESSION 4: REFUSE TO GET REVENGE

Optional Activity

Purpose: To help us learn alternatives to seeking revenge.

Activity: How might the following people respond to their situations without seeking revenge? Split your group up into three smaller groups and have each brainstorm next steps.

- Graham, who has worked tirelessly for his company for ten years, was overlooked for a recent promotion at work because the boss's nephew, who just started working for the company, was given it instead.
- Marion's neighbor put up a fence that extended over her property line. She tried talking to him, but he wouldn't listen. Her friends are encouraging her to sue him.
- Thomas, a schoolteacher, was falsely accused of a crime he didn't commit. The person who spread the rumors has long disliked Thomas because he was open with students about his Christian faith.

Teaching point three: Instead of seeking revenge, forgive.

[Q] How were you healed by Christ's wounds (v. 24)? Give practical examples.

[Q] What difference does it make to you that your sins are forgiven?

[Q] How does dwelling on what Christ did for you help you to forgive others?

[Q] What does it mean to die to sins and live for righteousness (v. 24)? Why do we need to do that if we have been forgiven for our sins by Christ's death on the cross?

Leader's Note: Although our sins have been forgiven because of Christ's work on the cross, we still need to confess our sin daily and choose to live righteously so as to not make a mockery of what Christ did for us.

[Q] How does Christ shepherd you on a daily basis (v. 25)?

PART 3
Apply Your Findings

Action Point: Ask each person in the group to think of anyone they need to forgive. Ask them if they need to take any action besides talking to God about it. Take a few moments for silent prayer for them to bring it to God. Close by praying aloud that God will give each person the strength to carry through with what God has shown them.

SESSION 5: LEARN TO LIVE IN PEACE

PART 1
Identify the Current Issue

Discussion starters:
[Q] What comes to mind when you think of having a good life? Describe it for us.

[Q] What kinds of things do you think most affect your quality of living?

[Q] What kinds of things would make your life the happiest?

PART 2
Discover the Eternal Principles
Teaching point one: Think about what you say.

[Q] How can we learn to talk less and practice silence? Suggest some practical ways.

[Q] What are some possible consequences of our words?

[Q] How might being careful in our words improve the quality of our life?

[Q] How can speaking rashly bring us to ruin (Proverbs 13:3)?

[Q] How can our words bring healing (Proverbs 12:18)?

[Q] In what ways does the tongue have the power of life and death (Proverbs 18:21)?

[Q] How would your relationships improve by you showing sympathy, compassion, and humility (1 Peter 3:8)?

[Q] How might it change your life if you bless someone who insults you (1 Peter 3:9)?

Teaching point two: Think about what you do.

[Q] Which of the following describes what our motive should be in doing good?
a. To be rewarded in heaven
b. To earn favor with God
c. To earn a place in heaven
d. To show my joy in what God has done for me

Why did you pick the statement you did? How does it motivate you to do good?

Leader's Note: a. We should be motivated by our heavenly reward, because it shows we believe God and are living for him. b. We already have favor with God if we have accepted his Son as a sacrifice for our sins, therefore we don't need to do more to earn favor. Such thinking can exhaust us because we never feel we are accepted by God. c. Another variation of b. d. As we fall in love with Christ, we will naturally want to please him. Love is the greatest motivator there is.

[Q] What are some practical ways you can turn from evil and do good?

[Q] Why are we blessed if we suffer for what is right (v. 14)?

[Q] How does it affect our behavior if we set apart Christ as Lord in our hearts (v. 15)?

[Q] How can we keep a clear conscience (v. 16)?

SESSION 5: LEARN TO LIVE IN PEACE

[Q] How might you do as Isaiah suggested and seek justice, reprove the ruthless, defend the orphan, and plead for the widow? List practical ways to do this in our society. Why do these things please God?

Teaching point three: Think about your attitude toward others.

[Q] Why is God attentive to the prayers of the righteous? What does that mean in practical terms?

Leader's Note: When we are living in a right relationship with God and in obedience to him, we are in tune with his Spirit and able to heed his guidance and direction in our lives. We will be praying for the right things, and God will delight in answering those prayers.

[Q] How will we be blessed if we suffer for doing what is right (v. 14)? Can you think of any examples of Christians who have experienced this?

[Q] How can we get over a grudge?

[Q] With whom do you need to pursue peace?

Optional Activity

Purpose: To help us learn how to be Christ-like in our relationships.
Activity: Pass out index cards and pens. Ask each person to write down a difficult situation they are facing in a relationship with someone, without using names. When they are done, pass around a large bowl to place the cards into. Instruct each person to draw out a card other than their own. Take turns reading them aloud and suggesting ways the person can show the love of Christ in this situation.

PART 3
Apply Your Findings

Action Point: Ask the group to make a commitment to improve their relationship with at least one person this week. It may require an apology, a letter of connection, a phone call, or an act of service. Remind them that you will ask them next week how it went. Pray for the individuals in your group to have courage in this endeavor.

SESSION 6: GET READY FOR A ROUGH RIDE

PART 1
Identify the Current Issue

Discussion starters:
[Q] There is a saying that goes, "God doesn't care what you go through nearly so much as how you respond to what you go through." Do you think that's a true statement? Why or why not?

[Q] If you have children, how do you prepare them for the tough things in life? How should we prepare ourselves?

PART 2
Discover the Eternal Principles
Teaching point one: Prepare your mind.

[Q] Why do you think Peter told us to "arm" ourselves with an attitude like Christ's? How can we do that?

[Q] What evil human desires (v. 2) are we tempted to live for? What does it mean to instead live for the will of God? Has anyone ever heaped abuse on you for trying to do that?

[Q] How can suffering help us to become stronger in Christ? How does it help us to better resist temptation?

[Q] Is faith that hasn't been tested valid? Why or why not?

[Q] Why should we rejoice that we get to participate in the sufferings of Christ (v. 13)? Why would that make us overjoyed when his glory is revealed?

Teaching point two: Prepare your soul.

[Q] What do you spend most of your time praying about?
    a. Forgiveness of sins
    b. Strength to serve
    c. Praise to God
    d. Asking for things
    e. Praying for others
    f. Wisdom and guidance

Why did you pick the statement you did? What do you think you should spend most of your time praying about? Why?

[Q] Why do we need to be clear minded and self-controlled when we pray (v. 7)?

[Q] How does our love for others affect our prayers (v. 8)?

[Q] Why is hospitality important in preparing our souls (v. 9)? Why should we avoid grumbling?

[Q] How does serving one another improve our soul life (v. 10)?

[Q] Why do you think Peter so often ends what he is saying with praise to God (v. 11)? How does such praise prepare our souls?

Teaching point three: Prepare your heart.

[Q] What do you think it means to "love each other deeply" (v. 8)? What are some practical ways we can do that?

[Q] What does it mean to be hospitable? How is that different than

SESSION 6: GET READY FOR A ROUGH RIDE

entertaining guests?

[Q] What do you think God has gifted you to do? Do you feel you are using that gift?

[Q] How can we learn to speak the very words of God? Does that mean we only quote Scripture verses? If not, what does it mean?

Leader's Note: Nothing is more annoying than someone who quotes Scripture nonstop. Christ and the apostles quoted Scripture occasionally, but they strove to always speak truth. We should make sure our words line up with Scripture, even when we aren't quoting it.

Optional Activity

Purpose: To help us learn to love others deeply by our actions.
Activity: Pick someone you know who is going through a rough time. Decide as a group what you can do to encourage this person. Each member of your group may be able to use what they are gifted at to help this person. Discuss it and come up with a plan.

PART 3
Apply Your Findings

Action Point: Break into pairs. Take turns sharing what needs to change most in your life: judging others or serving others. Take time to pray for each other concerning this.

PART 1
Identify the Current Issue

Discussion starters:
[Q] Is worry a problem for you? If so, what kind of things do you worry about? Do the things you worry about usually happen?

[Q] Have you experienced a time you trusted God even though you had a valid reason to worry? If so, tell us about it.

[Q] How do you handle it when you can't feel God's presence?

PART 2
Discover the Eternal Principles
Teaching point one: God will honor you if you humble yourself.

[Q] How can we act with humility toward each other? Give practical examples.

[Q] How can you tell whether you are being humble?

[Q] Why do you think God opposes the proud (v. 5)?

[Q] What does it mean that God gives grace to the humble (v. 5)?

Teaching point two: God will take care of you.

[Q] Which of the following best describes worry?
   a. Lack of faith in God
   b. Reasonable response to the stress of life
   c. Necessary to be prepared for life
   d. Unavoidable since we're human

Why did you pick the statement you did? How does that attitude affect your life?

[Q] How can God help with our worries?

[Q] What are some ways you have learned to cast your anxieties on God?

[Q] Why might what seems unloving actually be a loving gift from God?

Teaching point three: God will restore you.

[Q] What does Peter mean when he tells us to be self-controlled and alert (v. 8)? What would that look like in your life?

[Q] How can we recognize when Satan is trying to devour us?

[Q] What practical things can you do to resist Satan?

[Q] What does it mean to "stand firm in the faith" (v. 9)?

[Q] Why does it encourage you to know that others throughout the world are also suffering (v. 9)?

Optional Activity

Purpose: To give us a glimpse at how God can restore a life.
Activity: Divide into groups of three or four. Give each group a magazine that has a lot of pictures of people. Ask them to find a photo of someone, make up a story about that person that includes hardship, and imagine how God might restore him or her.

PART 3
Apply Your Findings

Action Point: Ask each member of the group to share the one thing they would most like to see God work into their life as a result of this course on 1 Peter. Pray together that God would help them to trust him for the grace and power to see that happen.

Made in the USA
Middletown, DE
01 March 2018